Acclaim for MAYA CHINCHILLA's
The Cha Cha Files

The Cha Cha Files: A Chapina Poética vividly documents, from multiple perspectives and positionalities, the experiences of forging and affirming new identities in the United States. Maya Chinchilla's cutting-edge Chapina poética eloquently and richly tells the varied histories, realities, dreams and desires of U.S. Central Americans. *The Cha Cha Files* is a must read!

> **Alicia Ivonne Estrada**, Associate Professor of Chicana/o Studies, California State University, Northridge

Maya Chinchilla's *The Cha Cha Files* is the Guatemalteca femme anthem and diary we have been waiting for. I love the way she meticulously documents and hopscotches through these precious, needed moments of queer brown girl memory, history and body. *The Cha Cha Files* captures the graceful power of Chinchilla's performances with a deft telling of these autohistorias on the page.

> **Leah Lakshmi Piepzna-Samarasinha**, author of the Lambda Award-winning *Love Cake, Consensual Genocide* and *The Revolution Starts At Home*

Maya Chinchilla's collection documents and dialogues with identity, home, remembering, and belonging in a syncopated dream language. You don't know whether to surrender to its perfect lyricism or pour meticulously over every word contemplating the layered meaning in the metaphors and memories. She writes with vulnerability and intention on the politics and inestimable complexities of Latinidad and indigenismo, queerness, gender, borders, and love. Finally, her work is a call to action to those whose stories remain untold: "Unless we document ourselves we are invisible!"

> **Virgie Tovar**, author of *Hot & Heavy: Fierce Fat Girls on Life, Love and Fashion*

The Cha Cha Files

The Cha Cha Files:
A CHAPINA POÉTICA

Poems by Maya Chinchilla
Foreword by Ana Patricia Rodríguez

Kórima Press

Credits: Grateful acknowledgement is made to the editors of the following publications in which these poems appear, sometimes in different versions:

"Solidarity Baby" and "Papeles/Paperless" appeared in *Desde el Epicentro: An Anthology of U.S. Central American Poetry and Art* (Los Angeles, 2009).

"Central American American" appeared in *La Revista* (UC Santa Cruz, 1999).

Early versions of "24th and Mission Border Transmission" appeared in *Toltecayotl Cihuatl*, Mujeres de Maiz Issue No. 4, and 13 *BAKTUN: Return of the Wisdom of Elders,* Mujeres de Maiz Commemorative Issue No. 8 2010, and *La Lunada: An Anthology celebrating sixty full moons of spoken-word poetry at Galería de la Raza 2004 - 2010* (Volume 1, 2010), edited by Marc Pinate.

"The Raw Stuff" first appeared in *Americas y Latinas* (Stanford University, 1998).

"Homegirl" first appeared in *Sinister Wisdom* 74, Fall 2008.

"Oh My" first appeared in *Las Girlfriends,* Volume 2, Number 2, 1999.

"Committed" first appeared in *Encantadas* by Las Manas, 2008.

"Central American Unicorn," "Red Puta Heels and the Joker," and "Baby Holds Half the Sky" (early version "Mama holds Half the Sky") first appeared in *Cipactli Journal* (San Francisco State University, 2014).

Cover Art: Yolanda Lopez and Rio Yañez
Title: Dreams of a Central-American Unicorn
Medium: Tempra paint and digital illustration

Author Photo: Rio Yañez

Published by Kórima Press
San Francisco, CA
www.korimapress.com

ISBN: 978-0988967380

To my parents, Norma and Jorge, and my sister Tanya, my origin story; my family both together and apart, for all your love, humor, and support, in abundance and upheaval; and for giving me a lifetime of stories.

Contents

Part IV. Cha Cha Files

Foreword

Maya, Illuminating Woman and Words

by Ana Patricia Rodríguez, Ph.D.

In the Spring of 1999, I had the good fortune to read Maya Chinchilla's poetry in the inaugural issue of *La Revista*, published by the University of California, Santa Cruz (UCSC). In that prescient volume, Maya premiered her groundbreaking poem "Central Americanamerican," which would give name to the diasporic cultural formation and field of studies known today as "Central American American." Even back then, Maya had *la facultad*, as Gloria Anzaldúa would have it, to speak from the wounds of trauma, ask the most painful questions, and imagine worlds for Central Americans born and raised in diaspora. Now, in her her long-awaited collection of poems, *The Cha Cha Files: A Chapina Poética*, Maya Chinchilla offers readers a cycle of poems, which continue to ponder Central American identity and cultural formation in the United States and to open new spaces for U.S. Central American literature.

Organized into four parts, respectively titled "Solidarity Babies," "Central American Unicorns," "Homegirls and Dedications," and "Cha Cha Files," Maya's collection of poems bridges the past and present, the historical and the imaginary, the poetic and the testimonial, and the Central American and the diasporic, posing these terms not as binaries but as continuums. In the first section, she reflects on a childhood spent in between cultures, countries, histories, and geopolitics that give shape and purpose to her consciousness, especially in her classic poem, "Solidarity Baby," in which she recounts attending marches and rallies in "a yellow baby backpack with a metal frame" atop the backs of her parents, silently watching "the Central American Underground Railroad" run "thru [her] living room," and "listening to proud Maya woman / mujer de maíz / using the conquerors language to testify / while Mami interprets." Witness to history and yet not quite the subject of it, the solidarity baby and others of the diaspora, "don't know what it's really like" to be Central American, whatever that may be essentially. In Maya's poems, what matters is not getting *it* right, but knowing one's place in the "long line of resilience"—the Central American resilience, if not resistance.

Hence, throughout Maya's work, all things Central American—names, places, persons, history, identity, among other things—are always uncertain things. "I'm just a solidarity baby / don't know what it's really like…." In her account, dictators, revolutionaries, and solidarity workers like her parents made plans, took actions, and told truths, while the solidarity baby was left "looking for [her] place" and asking "am I a CENTRAL American?" The questions as to what is Central America and who are Central Americans appear recurrently throughout Maya's poems. The "Solidarity Baby" comes to the realization that though the diaspora (the solidarity babies) may not share the same history and experiences as Central Americans in the isthmus, diasporic Centrals Americans have created their own space of belonging, "soy del epicentro," the imaginary site of poetic creation and political action. In the Epicentro, the solidarity baby, like the diasporic subject, wages battles, makes secret plans, takes action, practices "storyteller strategies," translates pieces, observes "what is not obvious," reports "truths untold," and documents that which has been rendered invisible. Indeed, as a whole, *The Cha Cha Files: A Chapina Poética* is an exercise in documenting and bringing to light the Central American diaspora.

Setting the course for this documentation, in "Central American-American," revised many times over since 1999, Maya asks pointblank:

> Centralamerican   American
> does that come with a hyphen?
> A space?

That space is the space of seven countries sharing a geophysical landmass known as the isthmus amid a wide diversity of peoples, cultures, histories, politics, agendas, interests, and visions of the future. Cultural critics like Dante Liano, Arturo Arias, and Maritza Cardenas, among others, have written on the cultural construction of Central American-ness inside and outside of the isthmus, pointing to the ways that Central America has been configured and imagined historically. In her poetic meditation, her *Chapina poética*, Maya points to the region as the site of imaginary be/longings for the Central American diaspora and asks:

> When can we rest from running?
> When will the explosions in my heart stop
> and show me where my home is?
>
> Are there flowers on a volcano?
> am I a CENTRAL
> > American?
> Where is the center of America?

In her ponderings, Maya echoes the *inquietudes* of the Central American diaspora: "Are there flowers in the volcano?" Alluding to the title of the solidarity classic by Claribel Alegría and Carolyn Forché, *Flowers from the Volcano*, Maya recalls that for many of the diaspora, especially those who came of age during the civil wars, Central America was pieced together out of the images, words, and impressions of clandestine books, resistance literature, and testimonios smuggled into our classrooms at campuses like UCSC. Did we really know our "homelands," or were they figments of our imaginations? Were we part of the struggle, or vicarious consumers of that narrative? Her words cut deeply into many of us—children of the Central American diaspora—trying to find our place in the world during the long civil wars (1954-1996) and their aftermath in Central America as well as the ongoing cultural wars (1989-1999) in the United States. In the 1980s and 1990s, we fiercely fought to find our voices and identities as

Centroamericanos. Now as then, the question of who / what are Central American-Americans remains a burning issue for the Central American diaspora. Raising the solidarity call to action and remembrance in the first section of her collection of poems, Maya explores growing up between memories, travels, parents, grandmothers' houses, tortillas and potatoes, the United States and Central America, English and Spanish, and "gender selection and imposition," as she puts it in the poem "Baby Blue, Pretty Pink." Tucked into this first section is a poem titled "Mayita," wherein we are made privy to a meditation on the "magnitude" of the name Maya, "illusion in Hindi," "dream of duality," "maker...magic," and "history of hombres y mujeres de maíz." The legacy of resilience and survival weighs heavily on the poet with "sturdy resilient women [who] were counting on me." So much so that, in "Baby Holds Half the Sky," the poet is forced to admit

> but along the way I would forget
>
> believe I was not enough
>
> hiding in the silences in between.

In the second part of the collection, "Central American Unicorns," particularly the poem "What It's Like to Be a Central American Unicorn for Those Who Aren't," the poet seeks the mythical figure of the Central American. This illusive figure is

only mentioned

if at all

in relation to war, trauma, maras, revolutions,

earthquakes, canals and volcanoes

Indians kidnapped by aliens, and

the Guatemalan maid as your punchline

but has her own story to tell

caring for your children so you don't have to

so she can care for children back home

because no one else will.

Truth be told, Maya's poems in this section fill in the losses, silences, lines, gaps, massacres, and disappearances in historical memory and give testimony to being "the only one of my kind," or rather the children of the diaspora who can only return to an "imaginary homeland." They must learn to follow the incense trails and read the hidden signs left behind by "other imaginary creatures." Maya keeps the copal and the light burning, illuminating the way to the imaginary homeland so that we can make it back home through her poems in this section: "Doña Maruca," "Guate Place of Trees," "No Nonsense Grand Ma Goddess," "Abuelito's Funeral," and "Hip & Roll." Armed with a "Chapina Dictionary," readers discover that the "solidarity baby" has become "a Chapina with an X on her chest like a super hero mayan intuitive espiritista getting a handle on her powers." We discover that the collection of poems is the story of the poet regaining her power and language. In "Maya Like the People," she is revealed as a

Central American superhero

powered on black beans, tortillas and el pueblo unido

radical loving rebel girl

sensitive but not breakable

two spirit open heart school girl humble diva

The poet assumes her lineage as one in the long line of resilient women bearing the weight of the world and the "ancestral knowledge" bequeathed to her by her parents and the Maya woman giving testimony to the world yet denied the word by those who would question the power of testimonio. As poet and storyteller, Maya assumes her role as "corny tamale palabrista," trickster of words, teller of truths, *"calling on the silence and making it loud."*

In the third section of the collection, "Homegirls and Dedications," the poet returns to "24th & Mission Border Transmission," the urban borderlands of migrant men in transit, passing time in the "bar on the corner," and women raped on both sides of the border. Illuminated by her *facultades* and the feminine light, the poet takes up her calling to call out *truth to power*: "¡No están solas! We are not alone," walking the streets of 24th and Mission, Guatemala, or Juárez. In "The Raw Stuff," "Femme on Purpose," and "Homegirl," the poet embraces "the (oppositional) flow" of her queerness, which in "Jota Poetics," she describes as a state of "full of living theory / and supported creativity" and making a "bless-ed home... soaring above the air / healing all who come in contact." In lieu of a homeland sought by the solidarity baby of the Central American diaspora, now the poetic subject joins the "la Jotería / speaking / broken / tongue harmony" in the ambivalent borderlands of all those without state, nation, language, family, and homeland. In these borderlands, all seek "the quetzal bird's necessary freedom ("Homegirl"), for which no papers, documents, "papeles," and rigid sexual norms and practices are necessary. In the third section, then, poet and readers arrive at the border and the poem "Walking Wounded," bearing old wars, norms, hurts, loves, fears, and cares that have left scars. In successive poems of this section, the poet explores healing through "Commitment" (fear of), "Hands Held" (love lost), and "Dedication Night" (abandonment).

Finally in the fourth section, "Cha Cha Files," the "solidarity baby" now a "poet in recovery" comes full circle, courageously facing the contradictions in her life. One moment she fearlessly seeks a lover who has "experience in bi-lingual mouth to mouth" ("Wanted"), embarks on travels thorough "tropical utopias" and learns lessons in "bicultural living" to outfit her Central Americancaness" ("PR Travels"), and finds pleasant reprieves ("Oh My") and communes with the spirits ("The Visit") along the way. But the path to utopia and peace is still mined with "un-aggravated brutality," discrimination, and victimization ("Armando Corazones"), unrequited desires ("Thirst"), broken hearts ("Red Puta Heels and the Joker"), shame ("Más y Más"), and love lost ("Showing up"). With the fourth section, the cycle of poems closes with a long list of unfulfilled wishes for healing, love, respect, harmony, mutual support, "exhausting possibilities," "collective progress," and "transnational decolonized" lives connected across borders. In her poética Chapina, particularly articulated in the last poem of the collection, "Nuestras Utopias," Maya reminds us that historical healing can only come by dealing with the past, speaking our truths, and "archiving our knowledge of pain, self-destruction, and manifest destiny" so that we can "dance, sing all the insight, vision, flesh, [and] document [all] you need to hear, see, touch, be." That is what *The Cha Cha Files* reveals through Maya Chinchilla's illuminating Chapina poética.

Ana Patricia Rodríguez
May 12, 2014
Washington, D.C.

Alegría, Claribel. *Flowers from the Volcano*. Trans. Carolyn Forché. Pittsburgh: U of Pittsburgh, 1983. Print.

Anzaldúa, Gloria. *Borderlands / La frontera: The New Mestiza*. San Francisco: Aunte Lute Books, 2012. Print.

Chinchilla, Maya. "Central Americanamerican." *La Revista: Papel Picado / Paper Cuts* (Spring 1999): 115-116. Print.

Menchú, Rigoberta with Elizabeth Burgos Debray. *Me llamo Rigoberta Menchú y así me nació la conciencia*. México, DF: Siglo XXI Editores, 1984. Print.

Acknowledgements

There are many in my life without whom this book could not have been possible. I give thanks to those who came before me and to those who risked everything in the name of justice. Thanks to those who believed in me, cheered me on, gave me guidance, created art with me, provided an ear, fed me, and loved me.

I am grateful to those who invited me to speak, write, perform and share my early works—my second favorite part about being a writer, second only to the practice of writing itself. I want to thank those who engaged and wrote about my early poems before I realized I was part of a larger conversation. To the newer generation of writers, thinkers, creators: you consistently remind me this work matters and continue to blow my mind with your connections and questions. To those who crossed my path but could not stay, no scarcity politics here. I will always wish you well, for there is enough to go around for everyone.

There are too many to thank by name here; too many I will forget. I will just have to write another book and if you stick around I'll thank you then. Regardless, know that my gratitude is never ending.

To la familia Chinchilla and the Stoltz family, to Kathy, Bill, Carmen, Kris and extended family for all things.

I especially want to thank the kind souls who read multiple drafts of this collection providing unique and invaluable feedback. There were many eyes and ears, but in particular I thank: Vickie Vertiz, a generous talent, meticulous eye and one of a kind homegirl; Wanda Alarcón, artist scholar conjurer, holder of femme-stories and unique insight; Amalia Ortiz, powerhouse poet and playwright with the right words at the right time; Lorenzo Herrera y Lozano, muse, firebrand and visionary.

To my maestros y maestras of all ages who planted important seeds, including:

Willie Perdomo, Thomas Glave, Suheir Hammad, Marc Bamuthi Joseph, Juan Felipe Herrera, Cherríe Moraga, and Sharon Bridgforth for craft, heart and the most life affirming and game changing workshop experiences.

To Sarah Guerra a powerful force, a creative strategist, an underappreciated, behind-the-scenes magician, a family-dinner-and-dessert for the weary and for a community of loyal followers, evil conspirators and circus queens. Amiga. Go, Spurs, go.

Rio Yañez, for making every moment an art project, for Chicano-Chapina post-apocalyptic-solidarity trading cards, cartoon intellectualism, ghetto-nerd-zine guides to the universe, arguments about commas and feminism. Friend.

Yolanda Lopez, a seer, muse, inspiration, trailblazer, funny, witty and kind. My favorite Chicana Feminist artist before there ever was such a thing.

Ana Patricia Rodríguez, for my first Central American literature class, for vision and understanding the hunger for justice, for critical conversations, for long distance mentoring. Your work is relevant, necessary and visionary. Gracias.

Elmaz Abinader, for tough love, poetics and the VONA community.
Patricia Powell, for generous, detailed feedback on the original thesis beast.

Rebecca Edwards, for intellectual encouragement and "queer subject time we desire."

Truong Tran for my first graduate poetry workshop and for seeing me through to the end.

Luz Vásquez-Ramos, LBC homegirl, rockera aventurera, Mexico City international strategist.

Raul el Vampiro Diaz, todavía haciendo del Terror. Chingas mucho. Por eso te quiero. Familia para siempre.

Eddy Alvarez, for Jota poetics, for mapping LA with love, for writing dates and bringing out the scholar poet in me. You and your work are an incredible gift.

Michael Hames-García, for refuge in Oregon to write, for profound conversations, for nourishment both delicious and inspired.

Central American filósofos y feministas: Leisy Ábrego, Karina Oliva-Alvarado, Suyapa Portillo, Alicia Estrada, Leyda Garcia, Arely Zimmerman, Oriel María Siu, Hector Perla, y Arturo Arias. I am in awe of your intellect, creativity and fire. Each one of you has altered my universe profoundly.

To my creative community:

Melissa Lozano, Lisa Marie Rollins, Kenji Liu, Aimee Suzara, Sara Campos, Ruben C. Gonzales, Chino Martinez, Leah Lakshmi Piepzna-Samarasinha, Julio Magaña Saludado, Cruz Grimaldo, Hugo Carbajal, Virgie Tovar, Julia Eden Ris, Sandra Garcia Rivera, Adilia Torres, Lito Sandoval, Chucha Marquez, Karla Marcela, Yosimar Reyes, Amir Rabiyah, Jaime Barajas, Baruch Porras-Hernandez, Nancy Aidé González, Hector Tobar, Darlene Elasigue, Nicole Griffin, Gracie Arguelles, Aleh Hurtado, Felipe Flores, Carmen Iñiguez, Connor Fu, Nia Witherspoon, Adelina Anthony, Dino Foxx, Anel Flores, Maricela Olguin, Madeline Lim, Kebo Drew, Liliana Hueso, Olga Talamantes, Galería de la Raza, La Peña Cultural Center, The Chicana Latina Foundation, National Queer Arts Festival (NQAF), Queer Women of Color Media Arts Project (QWOCMAP), National Association of Latino Arts and Culture (NALAC).

To the Magic Room Poets for showing up and sweating it out. Adobe Dojo, for practicing pure joy in the desert and a return to play and paper. Friday night writers, No Trigger Warnings writing circle, Church of Poetry, the Lunada Literary Lounge, Hybrid Performance Experiments, Epicentro Poets, End-Dependence, Rainbow Theater, Spanish for Spanish speakers, Sugarcane, Peacock Rebellion, Teatro Q, VONA Voices, Dos Brujas and especially to all the women of Las Manas: I carry your potent powers with me always.

Colegas for the opportunity to learn, teach and transform:

Clarissa Rojas, Teresa Carrillo, Nancy Mirabal, Bridgette Dávila, Katynka Martínez, Alejandro Murgia, Luz Calvo, Catriona Rueda Esquibel, Carlos Cordova, Andrew Jolivette, Gabriela Segovia-McGahan, Alberto Ledesma, Chela Delgado, Frank Galarte, Pedro Di Pietro, Cindy Cruz, Genevieve Negrón-Gonzalez, Sandra Álvarez, A De la Maza, Audrey Silvestre, Sara A. Ramirez, Jen Vaughn, Leis Rodriguez, Sayo Fujioka.

To my love: "Lil' foot" so generous, supportive, tender and willing. My heart.

To the Kórima Press family: thank you for this sacred work.

The Cha Cha Files

PART I: Solidarity Babies

Solidarity Baby

I'm just a solidarity baby
don't know what it's really like,
played on fire escapes
danced on rooftops
making fortresses out of boxes and paper plates.

My first march I rode above the crowd
in a yellow baby backpack with a metal frame
quiet and observant
I didn't cry or complain
'cause Mami and Papi were planning solidarity, baby
organizing dreams, taking on telling the truth
running the Central American Underground Railroad
thru my living room
my second-hand clothes given third-hand with first-rate love,
giving the little we had to those who had less
this is my inheritance.

While all I did was play with office supplies
and draw pictures of E.T. with highlighters
and learn to break dance in the halls
between the offices in front of MacArthur Park on 7th
drawing aliens playing with friends with aliases
wearing hüipiles for solidarity baby.

This one's for you Uncle Sam we don't want another Vietnam
This one's for you Uncle Sam we don't want another Vietnam[1]

I'm just a revolutionary honee
a product of an international relation
imaginary Guatemalan, porque *Guate no existe*
mistaken identity:
undercover gringa-chapina-alemana-mestiza
coming from a long line of resilience.

---

[1] From "No a la intervención" by Sabiá (English lyrics) and S. López (original Spanish)

Mamá, Papá, compañeros de los Centros de Información
extended family of activists
raising rebellious daughter
never doing as I was told.

I understand now that you being ahead
of your time means much suffering from it.
But it's beautiful to love the world with
eyes that have not yet been born.[2]

I remember hiding under literature tables
listening to proud Maya woman
mujer de maíz
using the conquerors language to testify
while Mami interprets.

I used to curl up on my father's lap while he
debated what lay between the lines,
Chapín Spanish booming from his chest, comforting.

I used to get names of dictators and leaders of the people mixed up:
Somoza o Sandino? Ríos Montt or Otto René Castillo?
Banana Republicans, Cold warriors Contras quién?
Was Reagan a good guy or a bad guy?
Let me see if I can get this right:

A-B-CIA-GIC-FMSLN-URNG-UFW-XYZ

I'm just looking for my place
am I a CENTRAL American?
Sí pues, soy del epicentro.

So what have I ever done for revolution, honey?
But entertain thoughts of clandestine self-righteous
militant explosions.

---

[2] "Before the Scales, Tomorrow" by Otto René Castillo

Si el poeta sos vos qué tengo yo que hablarte?[3]
I mean it's just a revolution honey,
why they getting so crazy?

I'm just trying to stay away from
letting them impose their guru on me.
Don't have to prove who's more down,
I'm just trying to keep my head up.

But, what have I ever done?
but survive race riots in high school
picking up the pieces using translator techniques
but get through college when the high school
counselor said it couldn't be done
but tell stories on a microphone,
possibly just touching one.

Compañeros míos yo cumplo mi papel luchando
con lo mejor que tengo.[4]
With the best that I've got.

No one knows my secret plans
documentary days, radio nights, printed palabras
what I am capable of
practicing storyteller strategies and messenger maneras
holding the door open for the little ones who are coming thru
what I am planning to do
it's part of my dynamically (un)disciplined destiny
to observe what is not obvious
risking reporting truths untold
layering laughter between tears
campaigning and complaining for the silent
who carry this country on their backs!

---

[3] "Si el poeta eres tú" by Pablo Milanés
[4] From "Viudo del mundo" by Otto René Castillo

Unless we document ourselves we are invisible!
there is so much left to do,
I'm taking on telling the truth
I'm just a revolutionary mama,
solidarity, baby.

The Meeting Game

(MAYITA, age 7, meets with her toys/associates in her bedroom/ boardroom.)

MAYITA:
(Yelling towards off stage at MOM.) I said I don't want to go. You can't make me. Moooom. I'm dooooiiiing sooooomethiiiing. Can't you go without me?

(MAYITA returns to her business.)
This is the first time I've been able to hold a meeting with my dolls and my stuffed friends.

Black ballerina Barbie made the agenda. She's the smartest of my dolls, you can tell 'cause no matter what I dress her in she always has that gold crown planted firmly at the top of her afro-puff ponytail. She didn't come with a name but we call her Kay. He-Man is staring at Malibu Ken who's always half naked in a bathing suit 'cause I don't have a budget for his wardrobe. I'd rather buy instruments for Jem and the one Hologram.

Yeah, I only have one of the Holograms, Kimber. So Jem and the lonely Hologram.

But the horsie contingent is well represented with all three of My Little Ponies, Miss chocolate love horsie, Mr. Unicorn, Peggy Pegasus who belongs to my sister, and Starlight, Rainbow Bright's horse is here. Rainbow Bright couldn't make it 'cause she had a previous engagement with a Transformer. So she says.

Then there's Carmen, my Mexican Cabbage Patch doll. I didn't get one when everyone else did 'cause I only get dolls on Christmases and birthdays and there was no way Mami and Daddy were going to stand in a line for some over hyped expensive doll. But then late one night Mami's friend Megan came to visit from Mexico and brought me one. She was dressed real simple in a puffy purple blouse, matching chonies, brown shoes and brown curly yarn hair. She didn't have bows in her hair or come in a box with a birth certificate or anything or come with papers like everyone else's dolls. But I loved her. My other dollies welcomed her and even shared their books and toys with her since she didn't have no-thing.

(*MAYITA whines towards off stage.*)
Moooooomm. Gah!

(*After a beat, she returns to business.*)
We have really important things to discuss, even my kittycat Cupcake is here taking notes and if I'm all the way at Gramma's house not everyone can go.

Gramma will make me do things like hold the clothes pins when she's hanging the clothes and will complain in that sing songy voice that I'm on the couch watching TV for too long. 'Cept she'll call it a davenport. Why does she call the couch a davenport? It sounds like she's calling it a porch or something outside. 'Cept it's inside.

At least she always has crayons and there's always some project going on in the party room. 'Cept there's never any parties. That's where Gramma's sewing is and Granpa's desk is. 'Cept he's never at it. He's always in the garage.

I like it when we go for a walk and sometimes we pick wild blackberries down by that school. 'Cept for the thorns. Hate it when I accidentally touch the thorns.

(*In a raised voice off towards off stage.*)
No I can't reschedule the meeting!

Why does my mom always try to make me go somewhere when I don't want to?

(To MOM.)
You should have checked with my secretary. What do you mean I didn't give you the right extension? The extension has always been 4567 and the area code used to be 2-1-3 but now it's 3-1-0. It got changed.

I hate it when Gramma tries to smooth down my hair. Maybe I want it that waaaaay. It's the style.

(To MOM now in the doorway.)
Oh Gramma's making chocolate pudding? Can I lick the spoon? Can I bring my Mickey Mouse record player? What about Cupcake? Can I bring her?

Oh right Gramma's dog Mario won't like that.

(In her meeting voice)
Meeting adjourned until next week.

Coming!

The Fremont House

At Gramma's house everyone has a job, especially when we're out of school. "No lazy bones jones in this house," Granpa says. He's in the garage working on his old style car. It's big and bubbly like one of those cars in the Dick Tracy movie. Sometimes he lets us go inside the car to look but not for too long. That car is not for play even though Mama says that's Granpa's toy.

I try to help him but if I even look like I'm going to drop one of his tools, cause it's heavy after too long while he figures out what he needs if for. Or if I put it back in the wrong place, even though he has clearly outlined each tool on the tool board so each one knows its place, he'll get impatient with me and tell me to go help my Gramma.

Gramma uses the fact that we are visiting to try one of her new church recipes on us. I'm good at helping, with following instructions. 'Specially if we are making dessert. If I'm patient I get to lick a spoon.

Gramma is old fashioned 'cause she spends way more time in the kitchen than Mama does, but she is also a very modern lady. She has all kinds of polyester pantsuits with matching coats and shiny blouses to go with each one.

Mama says it was very rare for grandmas to work like she did unless you were a secretary or a waitress. Gramma studied to be a Home Ec teacher and even took classes at night. That's why she likes to make things easy like using food in packages and uses the microwave to heat things up. She even heats up water for instant coffee in the microwave. We're not supposed to stand in front of it cause it gives off gamma rays or something like that. We're Lucky. Mama says they didn't have leftovers in her day like we do now.

If she wasn't going to be home she had to leave food prepared with detailed instructions so Granpa wouldn't starve.

I know I won't be able to eat dessert if I don't eat my vegetables but lucky we are going to have green beans from a can. They're real salty and make me lick my lips.

Gramma wanted to be a part of the modern world you know, try new things. But Gramma has to sneak onions or any spices, 'cause Granpa doesn't like onions or spices. Only salt, pepper and paprika. But I think paprika adds more color than flavor.

Instead of rice and beans like at my house, we usually eat potatoes at Gramma's house. Mashed potatoes, scalloped potatoes, whipped, boiled, small potatoes, big potatoes, baked potatoes, fried potatoes, potato pancakes. Sometimes, we also have pasta salad. But even the pasta salad has potatoes. Papas potatoes. Papas potatoes. Potatoes, potatoes, potatoes.

I wonder if that counts as a vegetable.

Mayita

Four letters I find myself spelling all the time.
Not Mía, Myra or María.
Easy to pronounce in any language.
Maya history of hombres y mujeres de maíz.
"Have you thought of the magnitude of such a name?"
"We Mayas don't exist. Yet here we are."

Maya is illusion in Hindi. *The illusion both blinds us in delusion and has the power to free us from it through consciousness. Dream of duality.*
Mama Buddah. Queen Maya. Maha Maya. Mayadevi.
Maya is the maker. She means magic.

Mayita. Little. Mijita. My little daughter. Mijamaya.
Papi jokes that he wanted to name me Mía. Mine.
Let everyone know I was his.
"Don't let anyone give you a nickname.
Make sure they pronounce it correctly
so your abuelita will recognize you when you are famous."

Once I met Maya Angelou and said,
"We have the same name!"
She looked at me and said, "So?"
Signed my book "Joy!" and said, "Who's next?"
Ayam Maya.

Baby Blue, Pretty Pink

the dance of gender selection and imposition
white bordered pictures of me in faded 70s browns, yellows, oranges

blood red turtle neck connected to periwinkle blue bell bottoms
tiny legs dancing underneath

mistaken for a younger brother with a non-specific bowl hair cut
even though I was wearing a skirt

anything boys can do
dancing back and forth

running kick towards the soccer ball
a common goal

salsa step back in line
lucky star sexy fleshy belly

cumbia liberation in sync with
gender bending soulful guitar riffs frilly purple prince tight pants

pirate shirt heels hairy chest
banda cowboys stomping over to my side where I wait with a

merengue free style and a roquera punch to the air doc marten solo step
link tribal rituals

who's leading whom
I can lead I can follow
and get down on my own

pink and purple I ran away from you when I found out what they meant
if I let on I liked girly things then you might expect me to regret
my tomboy ways

I had to be rough
tough
little miss hot stuff
don't trust,
don't open my door don't pay for my food, don't love me you fool
someday I'm going off to school
'cause love is for suckers.

Tres Pasos

1. Maya Mexica
   On first beat hit the body remembers
   chest lifts up to sky
   tentative beginnings
   ask permission

   feet talk to earth north west south east
   kids elders women men more spirits than names
   drum *boom ba boom ba boom bada bada bada boom*
   blood pulse heart time rhythm
   the dance is the conversation
   in body out of head
   ba boom ba boom ba boom
   ba boom ba boom
   bada bada bada bada boom baboom
   chapina among mexica

2. Chapín Jaliscience
   Folkoric gendered conversations
   colonial separations haughty hybrids
   rhythmic violins
   feet pound heel toe heel toe
   the zapateado step I never forgot

   she pounded into my head every day after school
   down grocery store aisles
   between burger and fries king taco
   in parking lots
   at the fabric store at the movies
   don't look at your feet stand up straight
   imagine nails echo sound from heels of shoes
   ribbon thread thru your spine hold up your head

   we danced for fun then to build
   after riots fired anger at convenience stores

took streets locked doors behind tv screens
nineties early spring
adult admin looked to fresh faces
for multi-culti bandaids
cause kids know what's up
know more about your kids than you do
we took scraps student assembled
tejiendo culture baile flor y canto
danced numbers
Azteca to Sinaloa to Rumba
to Caifanes Timberiche y Chayanne
dance the story
back to Porfirio Díaz dictated hyper Mexicaness

she was grace
victorian posture and ruffles
waist up Guadalajara tall
arms move skirt swirling half circles
slice air into waves
filling space with ribboned hems
no one remembers the names
of the men that danced around her.

3. West Coast Boricua
   Bomba puerto invitation rico
   repite: en la punta del pie
   women on the drum disrupting previous beat
   shaking out the flesh feeling new parts of body
   bay area communing together in the circle
   the call and the response
   the smile on her face when she says
   I loooooooove to dance
   both dreamy and assured
   muscle memory

grounded thru the hips chest arms elbow tip of foot
throw the conversation back to the drum
respeto release an africanborinquen survival story
te invitan or you jump in

4. On first beat hit the body remembers
   the way a bordered people travel forced
   movement pass culture teaching to young
   stand up tall lift chest to sky
   defy forced downward gaze
   bending over now for flexibility and strategy
   with lessons from a humble earth
   rhythm is your voice. Let her speak.
   Feet document story. Let them speak.
   Base boom. Let you speak.
   In the circle calling. Let us speak.
   Habla. The body remembers.

Baby Holds Half the Sky

I was born a bridge
a teeny tiny sickly little bridge
a plank really
didn't seem like I would make it
from one place to another
looked like a brief line in the sand

Told I could be ANYTHING
much more than my scaffolding
could challenge structures
bridge ideas
uphold a standard

Sturdy resilient women were counting on me
It's what we do   What is necessary   What we should

But you always worried about me
I didn't cry didn't complain
so quiet you could almost forget about me
fell asleep after one chi chi
took me so long to speak my first word

As a baby I traveled so neatly under your hüipil
several weeks after I was born
you   speaking on behalf of women from this continent
words careful   studied   not too proud
research from the ground

Competent women traveling internationally
conferring to build strategy and solidarity
serious business representing a hundred different countries
soften
when they see this tiny   milk   drunk   baby

So calm among the urgent
business of organization and influencing the powers that be
to save humans from top down policies
and
for babies
like me

So peaceful
I am passed around
comfortable in each woman's arms

Women smelling of earth and dignity
anointed in story

but along the way I would forget
believe I was not enough
hiding in the silences in between

The sky infinite growing heavy
I would need to learn my
bridge-building skills
can unite the terrain of me
freeing up time
worrying I was meant to fall

Would you know the weight I would carry
joining invented territories?
my fight with responsibility, duty and authority
my body's desires, my intuitive impulses would betray me,
my serious need to laugh at destiny and play with jagged edges

before I would finally give in   forgive   let go   have faith
let someone in   a little bit

honor much more than family
identity and
community

let me

let
you

love
me.

Central American-American

Centralamerican   American
does that come with a hyphen?
a space?
Central   America
America
América
Las   Américas

Español chapín
black beans and white rice
tortillas de maíz almost an inch thick
refugees and exiles
as playmates
movies with trembling
mountains, bombs and
gunfire raging in my heart.
black lists and secrets.
Hüipiles and mysterious people
passing through my home.

Where is the center of America, anyway?
Are there flowers on a volcano?

You can find the center in my heart
where I imagine the flowers never die

But today the volcano explodes in the way
it has every day for 30 years.
No it is not a sacrifice it desires,
for we already have sacrificed too much,

They want us out of this country
they say we don't belong here
vamos pa' el norte
they tell us the American dream is the truth

but that our stories of escape from horror are not.
When can we rest from running?
When will the explosions in my heart stop
and show me where my home is?

Are there flowers on a volcano?
am I a CENTRAL
        American?
Where is the center of America?

PART II. Central American Unicorns

What it's Like to Be a Central American Unicorn for Those Who Aren't
After Patricia Smith

First of all I am a mythical creature that is only mentioned
if at all
in relation to war, trauma, maras, revolutions,
earthquakes, canals and volcanos
Indians kidnapped by aliens, and
the Guatemalan maid as your punchline
caring for your children so you don't have to
has her own story to tell.

What happens if I never mention these things?
am I contributing to the loss
the silence, the erased lines
the gaps in historical memory
the opportunity for reconciliation
to make amends?

What if I never mention pupusas
or my grandmother's pepián, black beans and rice
or a quesadilla that's a cheesy bread,
not a tortilla with melted cheese
or the million ways to fry plátano
or Honduran baleadas, which I have yet to try?

What if I tell you that I am usually the only one of my kind?
that if I make up what is means to be Guatemalan-hyphen-American
no one in the room will be able to call me a liar?

What if I swear to all that is unholy
that if one more person shares that they went to study
Spanish in Guatemala and backpacked through the highlands without
ever mentioning massacred Mayans, the Quiché, the Mam,
the Ix'il, K'aqchiquel…
Yes "modern day" Mayans not kidnapped by aliens.

The "absence of" that is Ladino,
plus the Garifuna, the Mesquito, Pipil, Lenca…
not mysterious civilizations "disappeared."

Yes, thank you for knowing how *they* invented the zero
and no the world didn't stop in 2012
I don't want to hear about your trip unless
you are fundraising to get me and the diaspora
back on a regular basis.

What if I tell you I don't speak any indigenous languages?
(except for the remnants of words that have crept into the Spanish
I re-learned in high school when I went to Guate that summer)
That my family denies any indigenous ancestry
(though DNA and memory say different)
that we are an urban people who value engineering degrees
above all else?
that I haven't been "back" in ten years?
that there are silent wars among cousins and aunts and uncles
catholics vs. protestants vs. atheists vs. cremas vs. rojas
disjointed conversations of over here from over there and
over there from over here
and I can't go back over there in the same way anymore.
I can't go "back" there
over there doesn't exist anymore.

So I pack my Central American paranoia
that taught me everyone is shady until proven otherwise,
don't sit with your back to the door, don't count money in public,
leave your shoes next to the bed in case you have to run in the night,
remember walls have ears.

Mix in grains of sand from an imaginary homeland,
file them in a plastic file box and ride off to the next adventure
leave a trail of glitter that smells of copal, banana leaves, wood burning
stoves and moist green earth
so that other magical creatures may find me.

Doña Maruca

(Guatemala City, early 1980's. DOÑA MARUCA talks to her son Jorge while preparing a large meal)

I'm not complaining. I never complain.

So much left to do before everyone comes home for lunch. Tengo que calentar los frijoles, las tortillas, el pan francés y hacer las tortitas de carne. Yes everyone's coming. Para convivir con los Gringos. I mean, que estás ALLÁ. I can't even imagine what you eat over there.

Ni me digás, porque me voy a molestar.

Ay, Jorge, your little one Mayita. Everyone says she looks like you, hijo. With her gauzy black hair and those little dark sparks for eyes. You should keep her out of the sun. No es bueno para ella.

She looks like a boy, not a little girl, dressed like that. And how did you let her mother cut her hair so short así. Y esos shorty shorts. ¡No'mbre! You should tell her something.

No. Díle vos. A mí no me va a entender. Está muy agringada. Her tongue stumbles on Spanish like a baby who hasn't learned to walk.

Sí pues, if her tongue wasn't so floja I could tell her myself. Maybe she would help me with los frijoles y las tortitas de carne? If I wait around for her tongue to catch up we would never finish on time.

Ya estoy muy cansada, Jorge. Ya no aguanto esta vida. They say life is short but I think it's longer than I expected. I keep going because what would your papá do without me? Hay que seguir.

No es que no quiero a tus gringas. I love when you bring las niñas all the way over here to visit.

Y claro también quiero a su mamá. I saved all my monedas every week that one year to buy her that medallion. ¿Te acordás? I got it to protect her. To have a piece of Guate siempre and remind her of how much you mean to us. How much she now means to us.

I saw how you looked at her when she first came. I knew you were going to leave me for her. I knew when you went to Los Yunited you weren't coming back.

How could you leave after your brother died? How could you? I know it's been 18 years, but I never forget.

¿Y ahora con estas nietas gringas qué voy a hacer con estas?

They're growing so fast but they are still so young. You have to teach them how to behave over here. Tell them to forget all that "anything boys can do" babosadas from over there. You can't complain to anyone here. The police won't do anything for you. They are all corrupt and shouldn't be trusted. I want them to know this is their home too, but how will they learn that they can't just do what they want here? They keep asking if they can go to the street to play. I told them not to open that front door. What would I do if I lost them? So little. So "land of the free" inocentes.

You know, la Doña Dominga goes to pray every day for her son Elpidio. Four years of praying on her knees each bead of the rosario. He's never coming back, you know. Algunos dicen que en la Universidad se metió con la guerilla. He was studying to be an Engineer but probably someone put ideas in his head. And one day, without a word. Nada. Not even to say goodbye to know if he's dead or alive. Maybe he's fighting in the mountains for some lost cause.

You think I don't know what's happening out there because they don't show you on the TV. But I know enough. I don't have to be involved in la política to see what's happening. I know que es muy peligroso allí afuera. That's why we don't go to the campo or to las montañas any more.

Y estos militares bolos sin educación with their Gringo machine guns. Brothers fighting brothers while someone else controls the show and gossip is more reliable than the news. ¡No'mbre!

¡Y mirá! ¡Esta niña! I want to give her another bath. She's always getting dirty. I tried to scrub that mancha off her backside, so no one would think she was an Indian. That's what they say. Dicen que si tienés esta marca que sos indio o de Mongolia. ¿Te imaginás?

La gente habla de lo que esta pasando en el campo. Que matan a esta gente. Que por eso ayudan a la guerilla. Eso dicen. I know it's too dangerous here. It is probably best the time you went. So many of your generation are gone. Dead, disappeared or just nothing left inside because of the pressure. Who can you really trust?

¿Por qué no te quedás más tiempo?

Ay hijo, I can't go over there, allá, al norte. What I would do over there? No hay nada para una veijita. Y tu papá está feliz con sus loros y sus caminadas que hace aquí cerca. Los nietos que están aquí. Family and friends that are like family. That's what's important.

Come visit when you can, hijo. I'll send you your boots made the way you like them from the same place, como siempre. The leather and the smell of moist earth will remind you of home aquí en Guate. Just don't let those girls dress like Gringas. Keep them safe for me.

Guatemala Place of Trees

i.

Guate	bad
Guate	peor
Guate	buena
Guate	girl
Guate	chica
Guate	ixta
Guate	fea
Guate	bella
Guate	amiga
Guate	mama
Guate	sister
Guate	papa
Guate	mija
Guate	gringa
Guate	gone
Guate	guerra
Guate	maya
Guate	miss
Guate	mex
Guate	mix
Guate	sex
Guate	death
Guate	left
Guate	wrong
Guate	eternal
Guate	spring
Guate	prima
Guate	india
Guate	linda
Guate	ladina
Guate	media
Guate	boca
Guate	shute

Guate   triste
Guate   grito
Guate   oído
Guate   premio
Guate   centro
Guate   pasado
Guate   sangre
Guate   silence
Guate   story
Guate   myth
Guate   'xpress
Guate   freedom
Guate   libre
Guate   people
Guate   being
Guate   living

ii.
No existe
not existing
no exits
nunca existía

you are not
vos no sos
I am not
you are not
no seas
don't be a
don't dress like a
stand like a
talk like a
gringa
india(n)

puta
macha
loca
we are not
you are not
vos no sos
we don't do that
don't stand out
don't draw
attention
mind your
manners
don't embarrass the
somos decentes
no hablamos
así
las mujeres
no hablan
así
voseo
entre cuates
usted
entre los sexos
mexicanizados
hablas como
ellos
landed coulda been
Puerto Rican
Cuban Mexican Costa Rican
European (eastern western middle)
know who you are then
American hyphen
Central Central Central
American-American Central

American American-Centered
Central American Squared
Centro Centrical
Epicentro Epicentrico
Adentro Adentro in
Afuera Afuera out
Basque Spanish German Balkan
Maya
You insist not Mayan
media
half a Guate
half a dreamer
full of
Mayamor

que bueno
que vos
(entre nos
el sueño
our dreamer)
existís.

No Nonsense Grand Ma Goddess

1.
How to write you when we are always one
cycling through cutting in
unos cuantos piquetes
a few little cuts to bring your life force to the fore
bloody gory pools of bleeding four days
what makes a god what makes you holy what do gods bleed holy
no connection to any pure consistent benevolent all powerful gods or saints
no bloody Jesus mess no virgin flag in a glass case

Drunk off power usually involves the spilling
she who destroys
she who takes,
the time, to change
redeemer benevolent mother

Drunk on the spilling of a few little cuts
to be open, to be wound
cycling through
morning blood thick hot running till cold
copper offering to the grandmother of all

2.
My gramma never spilled anything
not blood
but rolled bandages just in case
she thick flesh tanned skin
she always warm
like hearth like bundle like cuddle like
she goddess of the practical
arms trunk-like
sturdy always put together

I dreamt of her smooth hair permanent wave set
pink lipstick click tongue clip-on costume jewelry polyester pant suits
she is river moving steady
packing a lunch prepping a snack she makes me think of lettuce
mayonnaise and potatoes
she the power of can opener and consistency
sing songy *time to gooooooo*
why didn't I hold her more often
she pat on the head and be on your way
never saw her cry never saw her fret
get your feet off the davenport
she well now, say, look here, not in this house.

3.
Makes me think the firey
who think themselves gods or goddesses spill blood
to show their power mark their territory, quién es más chingón
what would she do what did she do faced with these false ones
how did she become so sturdy.

Abuelito's Passing

"Mujeres no usan guayaberas," Abuelita says.

I blink across the table sending my dad eyelash distress alerts, but I don't know if he's paying attention.

Papá asked me what I wanted of Abuelito's, and those shirts are the only thing I want.

I wonder how old they are and where he would have worn them. The wine colored one is my favorite. The material is stiff and thick with white, shiny embroidery down each side of the breast pockets designs ending an inch before the hem. It is the elegant one, and I think of my stocky, desert-skinned Abuelito with his hearty laugh, travieso eyes twinkling, and soft-lipped whistling as he prepares for a family party. He pulls on the shirt one arm at a time, buttoning it up over a bright, clean Cloroxed undershirt, adjusting the collar and smoothing it out over his freshly pressed slacks, dress shoes shined, ready to swing my tiny Abuelita. She protests, "Ay, Maco," feigning propriety but secretly swoons at his overtures.

Her face crinkles and repeats, "Las mujeres no usan guayaberas," disapproving of this young gringa who must not know better.

I watch silent. My heart sliding down my intestines.

"No, Mamá. Son para mí." Papá dismisses her concern.

He's going to give them to me, right? Of course he will.

I relax a little and return to Abuelito's office where I am staying on the extra bed that sinks in the middle and the beige wool woven covers with the blue quetzal bird design that has been there forever. The room smells of years of humidity, like sticky, sweet banana leaves left to dry in the moist air. Clay floors tiled directly over the cement structure of the house reveal cracks from earthquakes and dignified age. The light is never bright enough. It flickers and reminds of a time when night signaled secrets and restless sleep.

I spend hours reading all the letters and old postcards Abuelito kept. One of the impeccably stacked boxes holds all of the letters my mom sent from California. They are tied with a faded green ribbon. Each letter is a time capsule. One describes who the farm workers were and why she wanted to work with them. She is unable to go down south on the freedom rides because she is sure her father will not sign the permissions. Another letter from Wisconsin comes enclosed with a description of a computer job my dad might be interested in and the kind of letter he needs to write in order to get an invitation to the U.S.

My dad says he's going to throw away the letters. What does he need them for? The only thing left from my parents' marriage is my sister and me. And the place he now calls home. That time is long gone. He doesn't understand why I would want to know about the past anyway. The past has nothing for you, he says.

I could have fought him but I don't want to cause him more grief. Not right now. Not this time. He lets me read them in consolation. I pour over them running my hands over my mother's perfect cursive before he mechanically erases their memory with the things that need disposal.

I try to stay strong for my dad. That is my role here as his assistant on this trip. I am his anchor, the one he can express his frustration to for not fulfilling everyone's needs. He is the patriarch now even though his older brother's death so long ago has always loomed large in Abuelita's sighs. His two sisters, each other's fierce adversary, one Evangelical and the other a kind of charismatic Catholic. Both want his advice on everything as if he will still be there in a few weeks to make sure everything is taken care of.

Soon he will have very little drawing him back to Guate and I start to feel my link disappearing. The Abuelitos' house was my Guate. My home base. The first place I imagine when I think about where I am from. You know. From from. Over there. The answer to the confused looks when someone studies my face and name.

In a few hours all the women will gather to recite the velorio in what is now only Abuelita's room, where he died. I will grow weary in my torn discomfort because I don't want to sit on my knees and I don't understand the prayers that well.

I learned Spanish better so I could talk to my Abuelos but I don't know if my Spanish was meant for praying.

Too Much To Be
"Si te dicen que soy más bonita que tú, no les creas." Ely Guerra

So I'm dancing all salsa step glad
the partner of the moment doesn't have sweaty hands.
And then the question
¿De dónde eres?

I stumble, why should I get tripped up on this question
What is he really asking
This a temporary relationship here.
We've only got one song. Loud music in the background
turns
around
how much attention will be given.

I'm from Long Beach.
Where?
I'm from LA.
Oh how long are you in the Bay?
No, I live here.
No but where are you frooom?
The Mission
I live in Oakland
You speak Spanish so well for a Gringa
I'm Guatemalan.

And then he says it.
You don't look Guatemalan.

That one, I'm used to.
My knee jerk reaction is to ask if he's ever been to Guate.
I guess at least he doesn't ask what part of Mexico that's in.
But if he'd only quit while ahead.
We've found a groove
Spins turns under and around.

Then he puts salt in the wound
But you're too pretty to be Guatemalteca.

Is that supposed to be a some sort of one drop rule colonial compliment?
I'm only borrowing beauty from a cinnamon Grandmother moon

boys are so stupid.
At least he didn't have sweaty hands.

Hip & Roll

a little rock
with a lot a rolls
all hips
with a bad case of hop
some country rancheras
cowboys singing the blues
with a polka beat

"échale salsita" merengaso
en la puntita cumbia son, punta com
African ritual seeping thru
my middle, my east
drumming my circle

third-world soul regurgitated
in to watered down pop tragedy for radio
rhythm in spoken words
storytelling from the soul
hummed sung vibrate through beat
good girls feelin bad
bad girls feelin good

a gansta rapper traced to the redneck
tribal line dancing repacked resold back to you

so underground you haven't even heard it yet
who will save the soul
of metalero rockero slampit tribal children
with holy rollers straight
no chaser like to goza del saborrrrr!
goza del dolor…

a little rock
a lotta roll

all hip with a bad case of hop
échale salsita merengaso punta com
no matter what station or planet you are on.

Chapina Dictionary

1. Ch (che) is the combination of consonants formerly considered a separate letter of the Spanish alphabet and used to be my favorite before they were so brutally ripped apart.

2. Siguiendo el criterio de la Real Academia Española, se ha envuelto en la 'C' según las normas de alfabetización universal. Su nombre es che.

3. Ecus me, su nombre fue che.

4. Some of my favorite words use these letters that make this sound. I used to use this letter at least twice when spelling my last name. I'm going to miss you cha cha, che, chi, cho, chu and sometime chuy. You're still my favorite even though now we are apart. You may be gone but never forgotten.

5. Ch is for

Bi-cho, Bo-chin-che, Boo-chí,Ca-che-ta-zo,Ca-chim-ba-zo, Ca-chi-va-ches, Can-che

cha cha, chafa, chale, chamba, chambiar, chambón, champal, champurrado, chanfles, changa, Chapina, chapucero, chavalos, chavela, chayote, chela, chele, cheli, chi chi, chica, Chicana, Chichicastenago, chido, chifla, chiflar, chingona, chingón, Chilango

chilaquiles, chile, chilero, chillaxin, chillón, Chinchilla, chingators, chipilín, chiple, chipis, chiquitica, chiquitita, chirimoya, chisme, chivo, chó, chocolate, chol, chola

cholas, chole, chompipe, chonchito, chones, choos, chorreada, chortes, chower, chucha, chucherías, chuchi, chucho, chuco, chula, chulos, chumpa, chumpe, chunche, chunchucullo, chuño, chupa, churro, churute, chau chau, colchón, colocho, hecho y derecho, macha, muchacha, muchá, púchica, no me touches, ticher, me pinchó.

6. A Chapina with an X is a Guate girl adopting the X, for what is lost, for the way she has been adopted into secret societies of Chapines, Chilangos, Chicanas, Chilenas, Tejanas, Salvis, Cubiches, Catrachas, Nicoyas, amantes de lola , and X for reclaiming, for the loss of the Ch, X for crossroads, X as in ch, sometimes X as in sh, as in Xela, as in X to break the shhhhh, I love all my exes, exis for x's. The X mark on hand that washes off after a night of dancing. A Chapina with an X on her chest like super hero mayan intuitive espiritista getting a handle on her powers.

Maya Like the People

Central American superhero
powered on black beans, tortillas and el pueblo unido

radical loving rebel girl
sensitive but not breakable
two spirit open heart school girl humble diva

the breaking point
the verge
the edge
emotional living on the surface
defender of the universe

a curvaceous activist
with warrior's insight
planning and multitasking

big heart love protected by a force field of
preparation and ancestral knowledge
living with a broken tongue
remembering what I love

that first time that first word that first kiss

love in the time of AIDS, riots and bilingual hate
heart break back beat floating down the river of
several rhythm nations

the topic of gossip and misinterpretation
my matrix jumping ways make you nervous

tough stuff sweet heart big dreamer
corny tamale palabrista
calling on the silence and making it loud.

PART III. Homegirls and Dedications

24th & Mission Border Transmission

Mi querido 24th and Mission
Conjunto on a Tuesday night
Mostly men gathered around to listen to the upright bass
Acoustic guitar drum and of course-- the accordion
Harmonizing reminding stocky brown skinned men of home

They will be home soon they think,
no need to do anything permanent here

And the bar on the corner always a
pop song, ballad, cumbia
salsita BLARING
The music sometimes draws me near
but the Men spilling out to the street ...ssst sst mamacita

Reminds me that no mujer decente would be in there
Some reason I know to walk away, (hurried hips try not to sway)
And even though I've never considered myself especially decente
and even my father says
I sometimes talk like one of *those* women in *those* bars
And we automatically know what one of those women are.

Poor women aren't allowed liberation
Or maybe they find freedom in tight jeans and
A stretchy v-neck that shows every bump every movement
Dripping ornaments dangle teasing
gold hoops lasso your eyes
You will see me!
Ay! He says, why do you women wear a dark bra under a white shirt
Only Nacas do that!

She sighs uncomfortable in skin she thought she was comfortable in
She thought it looked fine,
hurls back: that the bra is pink and is close enough to her skin!
as she changes to a darker shirt

They say don't walk alone at night because something
might happen to you
And if it does, well then you shouldn't have been alone

Blame the victim reflex,
so you don't have to take any responsibility
What if you don't have someone to walk with?
Lock yourself inside until someone comes for you?
Until the world changes?

And he says *yeah the world is a dangerous place for women*
but how are we supposed to change things?
It will always just be dangerous for women to be alone.
Some men will always rape some women.

I can't believe he says this, but then that is what we are talking about,
right?
Fear
the ultimate power over a woman.

Rape
Confidence busted
trust gone disgusted
picked up from a black top smack down
sub standard practices
negative in the place of a positive
accusatory sin and no redemption in sight.

It's dangerous to be a woman; even first world.
That is why I am connected to my hermanas on the border.
I know what it is to fear to have body of mujer
Be careful I hear they are killing women over there
My 1st world status means nothing?

Body parts, cut nipples,
legs disconnected from hips

Her brown eyes, her smile never seen
her laugh not heard anew
The last her mother saw of her was bone.
She didn't get to say good-bye.
Bone. No flesh to be ogled wounded.
What she most wants to hug her daughter again.

The Border
this line that is not a bridge, not a line, it's a ditch a hole an open wound,
like the Berlin wall the great wall of China, apartheid wall, imaginary
walls
not just one wall
but several, cement, iron gate, barbed wire
men with guns protecting who again?
Whose interests?
Eerie walls of silence

So we march, mourn,
we don't forget,
write letters, make speeches
hold discussions
Looking up from fear
and hopelessness
raising awareness
daring to be powerful

The Missing turned up raped & mutilated,
ni una más

Ineptitude bungling of local authorities,
ni una más

Blame the victim reflex
she must have run off with a boyfriend
maybe your precious daughter lead a double life.
Ni una más

Young, pretty, long brown hair, poor, brown skin.
Ni una más

Guate Mala Guate Buena país eterna primavera carga nuestra pena
También Mexico lindo y querido has some dirty secrets,
yes la madre de las tierras is helping hide our dirty laundry
out in the dessert, only half hidden,
so you know what happens to women who step out of line,
out of the house
NAFTAS's neglected, unprotected, migration survival,
maquila women earning 4 dollars a day
working on electronics, working on clothes she could never afford.

Explosion of exploitation!
Is only the half of it
Representing the condition
of women across the planet

Symptoms of a deeper problem.
Tener cuerpo de mujer es ser
amenazado de muerte
Her only crime, being a woman
Crimes against all our humanity

Pero sabes Qué?
¡No Están Solas! ¡No Están Solas! ¡No Están Solas!
We are not alone.

The Raw Stuff

I came
(thinking) (that I)
with my, ordinary wetness
was just a silly moisture, at best
but once inside,
I found the feminine fruit;
a la Frida Kahlo,
spread out,
on the table
like I wish I could do,
with the forbidden fruits in my silence.

I, Güatermelan, dripping
more water than melons.
hoochie feminist
with my máscara of mascara
and lipstick war paint.

Not yet knowing how to go about it,
I begin with a foreplay of mingling connections
and questions
networking my oppositional way to wetness.
taking up my pen I speak
penetrating
the paper
with slow, steady strokes and kisses
of thought.

But she said there is nothing romantic about
being an artist
that's okay. We've already romanticized a
Chicano or two-
It's time to romance and whip into shape the
slashed dashed space
between Chicana Latina.

I share with you some food for thought:
me,
a slice,
sweet and ready to quench your thirst.

Ooh baby, but I don't think you want to swallow
the seeds
a güatermelan might grow from your
womb.
Savor my taste
and come out
with your own recipe
for visionary theory.

With us she shared her hüpil space
crouched I saw a woman and was asked to tell
a story of what I saw:
My grandmother, my mother, sister and especially myself
nalgonas, nalgonas todas.
I hear that the personal is political
and I must make my political space public,
public, puh-bic, pubic!
Personally, I want to take my political pubic,
and my pubic political.

Bad thing she said, they were practicing abstinence.

So cut off your head
and open it up
take your nostalgic imperialism
and create the little miss attitude within you
your first salsa, dancing on your tongue
your first kiss, with ideas
your first time, masturbating
your mind.

Ahh! Finally, necessary wetness,
even without a token love poem.

So in the afterglow I realize:
that you should dip your fingered feet,
if you must, take a taste at least,
but, mija, don't be afraid to get wet
even if you have to go against
the (oppositional) flow.

Jota Poetics

Broken tongues speak
jotas into harmony
full of living theory
and supported creativity

Communing thru generations
with break of dawn conversations
dancing thru the night
dodging neon lights
sweating out the trickery
blinking back tunnel visions
remembering our whole selves in ceremony
with new ways of defining healthy

We are a bless-ed home
warmed by unexpected guests
we are voice
soaring above the air
healing all who come in contact

We are el conflicto rico y dolor
making-love-making-conscious
our praxis

We are loss
found in your forgiving arms
we are mystery
la gente
the lonely
a prison block
fighting to keep the mind free

Defiant vulnerability
precious
with a reinforced foundation

We are the threads that weave
a bed for you to lay
the wild roots that can't be cut back
the skirts of a volcano con su boca ebullada
the cactus flower blooming in the desert

We are letting go
holding space for the "mmm" not yet named

We are the ones
la Jotería
speaking
broken
tongue harmony.

Papeles/Paperless

i. Allá

He always dreamed
so he picked up from his 'go nowhere'
musician situation

She never sat still
And was that find language on the pillow country-by-country estudiante

He complained *gringas don't know how to put themselves together-*
All fodongas y flojas

She laughed hard when he said he was a feminist
'Cause he would protect a woman from a beat down

She just wanted to be friends
He had too many groupies

She always had time for everyone and everything
He liked waiting for her so he could watch her rushing to see him

He spent the night, but slept in the other room
He hoped she'd come back soon
And told her he'd come visit the U.S.
She thought that's what everyone says

They wrote letters and postcards 'cause he didn't have a phone
She always thought about the future
He didn't think he had one

ii. Aquí

She wasn't sure she wanted to go out that night, but her friends thought
she needed a break from school and a break from work.
His friends thought he needed to get out more, after two jobs and night
school

She saw him and couldn't believe it:
Was that her roquero on her dance floor?

He saw her and couldn't believe it:
Was that his little estudiante?

She taught him to dance as if he was squashing grapes with his toes.
It was the first time something good had happened to him in the U.S.
For the first time she let herself get all desperate and dramática

Two weeks passed and he asked her to be his girlfriend
all formal y la chingada

For the first time he wanted to be domesticated
and thought the moment-to-moment planning might be enough

With love in her heart and justice on her mind
She thought she'd use her birthright to save him
save herself
a ritual
a sacrifice
to show her love was down

iii. Ceremonia

She bought her dress at the mall with her dad.
He bought his first suit.

All present felt the magic in that simple moment
When she saw tears in his eyes she knew he really loved her
He said he always would and used 3 languages to make sure
She loves to cuddle all day but remembers she has to fill out all the
paperwork

iv. la ruptura

'Cause the immigration lines kept getting longer
They pay into a system that guarantees nothing
The lawyer said the Unabomber and 9-11 set off the laws that might
separate them

It's been 10 years and he wants to see his mama.
10 years and she pretends to keep the hope for both of them.
He threatens to go back even after all they've spent on lawyer-ing.
He says don't sympathize with his situation
'Cause he already feels like shit for causing so much trouble.

She knows what she did was right but still feels wrong
She wonders why she falls apart so easily given all those opportunities

She says everything will be cool.
He says nothing has been cool since.

Walking Wounded

1. an injury to living tissue caused by a cut, blow, or other impact,
typically one in which the skin is cut or broken.
2. inflict an injury on (someone).
3. past tense: wounded

you come to me with your open wound and i drop
everything
because this time i can fix it   fix you
and in the process i will be healed 'cause
i will finally be successful at something   you,
you will be that something, i think
and i will stand back and admire my work   you,
you will be that work of art and i will be your savior
your hero   your smart girl   the one who has it all
together the one who knows   this wise old soul
trapped in this baby's body.
i will be whole happy and ready to fix the next problem-
turned-project-turned-work-of-art

but of course that isn't how it is   how it should be
i get lost in you. i don't fix you.   you need even
more of me   i lose me   i drop me   i am gone
and you get lost in me too.
you hate me for wanting to fix you for thinking you need
to be fixed   for helping   you don't appreciate it   you
hate that i know so much   you put me down because
i know things you don't,
you criticize you tell me i don't know. you wish i was better
          more whole   that i did things the way you would.
that i don't fix.
i open up the wound   and explore how you got it
you tell me about all your tragedy and i want to heal you
'cause i know i can if you. let. me.
if i forget about me   if i forget about me i don't have to
deal with me

or my wounds   my mistakes   my fears my breaks
and well
i am the wound
you are the wounded
we are the walking wounded

Commitment

I'm committed
to staying away
from commitment-phobes
I need to be committed
     for dating your ass

I want
     with out
          having
               to
                    perpetrate the pass code
                    my affection the game

I want
     the stretch
     to let   go

Dig in for the long term
Don't be jealous of my gustos

I want it to be right   not   right   for   right   now
or together forever because
that's
how we're taught

You find the ones committed to be such a liability

We don't commit because we think there's something better
     I got your something better
          right   here
     Your move

Hands Held

Te escribo en español
porque entenderás
mejor

tus ojos te fallan
no ves bien

dices que
tuviste que estudiar
a escondidas
lápices robados
libros prestados

tus manos todavía
estremecidas
entre las cursivas

tú siempre a la defensiva
nunca olvidando
abuela que dio la espalda
acordándote de tu posición
tu papel como su mujer

huiste buscando mejor vida
o simplemente vivir
a la vez salvando y
perdiendo tus hijos

aquí
encontrando lo mismo
bruto y huele a alcohol

hoy
la sudadera come tu carne
esconde la mujer

so no one will threaten
like back then
when he showed you a ditch
the size of you and your children

your hands
have held babies
yours and others

held him back
losing

held spatulas
tortillas, cutting boards, punch cards, form letters
his freshly cleaned calzones and folded clothes of strangers

held tear drops
held body shakes
fear of small places

defiant
held tongue

held fake papers
broke(n)
promises

he said he'd give you real ones
held you captive to a break in the system
never ever

holding still
or star shine
free time,
daydreams
new hope
past lives
heartbreak
or song lines

breath shallow
lonely but
no longer
running from
an empty bed.

Dedication Night

I've taken to singing myself love songs
because there is no one left to sing them to me

the last romantic contender
I asked if we could pause
when I gasped at the view
from the top of the hills
of East LA skyline
perched behind mismatched concrete boxes made home
with winding plants
clay virgen guadalupes
guarding gardens with year round twinkling lights

At the stop sign I put the car into park
turned up the oldies
began to sing into my imaginary silver microphone
with multicolored iridescent streamers

It's just like heaven being here with you
You're like an angel too good to be true

I sang to you as if I lived it
as if nobody puts baby in a corner
as if our two girl love was about to have our own boulevard nights
cruising the strip in a fast car
going low and slow
and the sirens from a block over and the helicopter overhead
could never drown out my need to croon to you
mixing song pronouns as I pleased
from the depths of my shy girl letting loose soul

but when I opened my eyes to see if a kiss might be my prize
you rolled your eyes around and sighed as if you
didn't have time for my cliché overtures
I tried not to withdraw my offering

tried not to act disappointed
pretended I didn't see this as a sign
that this
would be over in a few weeks time

And so I sing every co-dependent love song
at every stop sign
twisting them into a dedication night
that lets me
love me
harder
than I ever have before.

Angel Baby. My Angel baby.
Oooh ooh I love you Oooh ooh I do.
No one can love me

Like i do.
OOOOOOh Ooh Ooh OOH OH
No one can love me like I do.

Femme on Purpose

1.
Words tattooed like nightmares
puta, perra, traidor, mojada wetback, fucking weirdo,
cunt whore, you're not a woman, pinche drag queen,
tranny, fucking freak, jota, maricón,
fucking bitch, get out of my way you fucking bitch

She yells these words crouching down
in my classroom
looking each student in the eye
hissing and taunting
not letting them settle into their seats
for their "introduction to trans 101"

Looks of shock, confusion, disgust,
recognition, discomfort, sadness
blink back at her
dart over to where I am seated
my back turned to them
so they can't search my face
for approval or comfort.

This is a taste of what I experience every day
Walking these streets, on the bus, going to school,
on my way to work, in the daytime, at night.
Every day I step outside to the judgments, projections and fears
reminding me of my place.
I tire. But I never let it break me.
My spirit has weathered too much for me to ever let down.

And every lesson about migration, gender violence, homophobia,
the patriarchy, economic inequality, I have concocted to produce
discussion
comes screeching from squiggles in their notebooks right into their face
speaking a language that calls both mind and heart to the discussion.

They can't look away
hide in text book descriptions
or parrot back to me essays of what
they think their profa wants to hear

Before them, this tall hazel-eyed mujer
with shades of walnut hair
frame indigenous features
full lips form every lilt of word
some careful and determined
some soft and hopeful
some matter of fact and biting
her laugh cuts through any sorrow

Students' eyes wide and careful,
stumbling polite words to get it right.

*What else do you want to know? Do you want to know how I do it? Where
I put it? Who I let hold me? What my status is? Are you thinking about it?
Do you want to know??*
Cause I do.
*I want to hear it all. Don't be afraid. Now is not the time to hold your
tongue. Here I have the time to speak back for each time they tried to
break me, steal my humanity.*
I won't judge you. I won't hurt you like they hurt me.

She weaves stories of being tied to a chair
until she washed secret stash of makeup from her face,
or rejected dreams of dresses and tight jeans
played with socks stuffed under blouses to imitate curves
her mama told her were not for her

Her father snuck her dolls, knows she likes pink
whispered *mija, tú eres mi hija*
when her mother was out of earshot

Her brothers stop walking with her to school
ran up ahead so no one think she belonged to them

She didn't sell her body over there. She worked
in second hand clothing store,
adopted by fairy godmother who showed her
how to contour the edges of her face
friendly con las chicas de la calle but didn't want that life
wanted to go to school wanted a career
had a boy friend who took her shopping and to the movies.

2.
After class over Chinese food in the Castro
proud of every English word she can use
to order her spring rolls and chow mein.
She says *ask me anything.*
Do you want to know what I've had done? I earned every cut.

I think how my own body has been under
attack on these streets the way men have whistled
and sneered and even hissed
nice tits, want to fuck? I want to cum all over that ass!
while walking two blocks from my car on Capp street to
queer cumbia where I think it's safe
to be a sexually actualized mujer.

Catcalls regulate who belongs where and how and when
no matter how many degrees or dollar signs I add to my name
safety is something I always have to think about
old wounds leave scars on my psyche.

But I will never know what it is to have been beaten
unrecognizable for the body of mujer that is still being sculpted
that is emerging from these stories like a song in rehearsals ready to sing
practiced polished, almost effortless.

She says *ask me anything*
I tell her I want to hear more about your boyfriends.
Do you believe in love? How are your English classes going?
Do you like your new job as a health promoter?

The things I've done for love.
The things I have to do to survive en este país

She scrunches her nose
Tú no eres lesbiana si te gustan las butchas
mujeres masculinas or trans men, she says to me.
she worked so hard to be the woman she is today
she can't imagine falling outside the lines of gender on purpose.
A propósito.
She says she's *always wanted to know what it was like to kiss a woman.*
And we laugh.

I am patient with my own stories
what is under the dressing I present
That my queer is on purpose, that my femme is on purpose,
that it was earned with discovery doubt self love
like she did.

Never found a boy that could make love like a woman,
although I tried. I tell her
loving women is like loving myself times two.

Queer is a funny word.
Hard to say the vowels get caught between the lips and teeth
the R falls silent when she speaks it
We don't have a word to translate what queer means, she says.

4.
You know femme was never about clothes, the presentation of the box
or who holds my hand

My femme has wild teeth, has tomboy roots, ragged nails,
has scars from sliding into first base
dresses ripped by clumsy boys, fights nightmares of war stories
the hard shell of my femme holds sweetness, caresses bruises,
and rings knuckles in case I have to fight my way out of danger
thinks but can I run in these heels if I have to?
My femme flags queer with nail polish and glitter, the books I read,
makes friends into family raises my own eyebrows at gender,
the way Oakland queers express themselves with their asymmetrical
hair cuts fashioning radical politics out of ironic t-shirts community
gardens,
fanny packs and neon leggings from my youth,
wears slacks and bright lipstick to work

My femme has put my tomboy to bed,
knows how to take pain that is wanted,
negotiates the terms consenting sexy
whispers *yes yes yes.*

My femme's been beat down from self hate, the *shoulda couldas* in my
rearview, the wound is my trophy, the fierce in my soft armor,
digs bare feet into earth calls moon to chest ocean wash request
dresses up sadness with sequins, fake flowers to the hilt when I want to
shake off the cobwebs–
and cleavage that begs *come on please*
I dare you to.
Even these chichi's are political.
Exactly as I should be.

5.
She didn't come to this country to sell her body
so she could get the body that she wants
this is not the story she came here to tell me
It was a job. Some give it away for free. I got paid for it, she says,

don't ever feel sorry for me. That's the worst offense you could offer.
The rest doesn't bother me. My spirit is stronger than it ever has been
before.

This is how I learn femme solidarity
reflected femme fierceness
from women who've earned it
who are different
who are femme
on purpose
just like me.

Homegirl
After Cisneros

You
bring out the homegirl in me
The one who has your back
My inner cha-cha chola
The big hoop girl
burgundy lips and sticky gloss kisses

The chingona intellectual
Who'd write the hoochie feminist manifesto
who'd cut a bitch just to see you again

La "Sí pues,
vos sos mía! A la gran púchica!"

That broke ass love
that novela chick that keeps coming back
the "if I can't have you then no one can!"

That gender deviant femme drama and butcha trauma
the Diego *and* the Frida
the ones your Mama (shoulda) warned you about

The steam from that jungle heat
the jaguar queen and jade obsidian

The social butterfly turned homebody
the queztal bird's necessary freedom

> I'd give it to you
> 'cause homegirl
> You bring out that
> *puta-madre-más-cabrona-punk-ass-bitch that don't need nobody*

> But just
> has
> to have you.

PART IV. Cha Cha Files

WANTED

Artistic Asthmatic
seeks smart, secure &
sweetly intense
lover
to carry her respirator

Love should be quick &
sneaky,
hitting without warning
Must take my breath away

Careful not to suffocate,
need
space
to
breathe
no cure for your love

experience in bi-lingual mouth to mouth a plus

PR Travels

A solidarity baby travels
at the speed of yesterday

Encounters paradise and traffic jams
hammocks for dreams and love-making

Pot holes and roads
rarely traveled

Heavily policed secondary sexualities
sun-stroked economic hustlers
beating down on imaginary countries

associated states of yearning and just getting by

Nationalistic flag waving-
light blue for independence

Don't forget Puerto Rico:
where bilingualism
gives me hope of tropical utopia
Strangled in American dollars

Faulty freedoms come at a price
blockading temporary travel for Cubans
stifling intellectual interchange
enduring temperamental
transnational transgressors

In Puerto Rico where:
legacies of Caribbean pirates
dance on the sand to salsa backbeats
while rebellious dancehall reggaeton anthems
shout from street corners.

grinding, slapping bodies *menea menea*
releasing tensions
instead of dancing around the issues
from this pressure cooker of ownership

Air conditions, conditional flows
get me stuck in random colonial moments.

In Borinquen
I revel in mixed conversations
flirt with community and temporary Latino-ness
juggling my own schizophrenic bridge making

Ruptures in my Centralamerican-ness
forging a traveled identity and
incorporating
generational self knowledge

Timeless transitions
recognition in bicultural living
seeking Rican-struction to call my own

Oh my

I like to sneak peeks
at you sneaking peeks
at me when we pretend
to sleep.
the universe in your hands
when you hold them
close to me.
in that moment in your eyes
I am not afraid to let me adore you.
but you sometimes look away
reminding me that there is uncertainty
in the future of love.
I want to release myself
inside you completely forever
even if only for one night
our legs touch
your fingers kiss my cheek
and your lips tickle my heart
sending shock waves through my hair

should I roll over
tired but can't sleep
I don't want to
wake you from your
silent dreams resting;
maybe when your eyes open
you will have the
strength to devour
me with your
whole soul
and body
and mine will
quiver with
exhaustion trying

to catch my breath,
breathing you
in, ready to climb inside
again,
not giving anyone the chance,
I prefer to tire you out myself.
and you smile in your dreams
while I wake
and am left with the smell of you sweated into my skin

The Visit

The spirits have been talking
and I need to learn to listen
they visit, sit, cry with me to sleep
wake me in the middle of the night
shapes of you enter my dreams
they know I'm not ready
your life has consumed me from the day we met
Ancestors ayúdenme!

We were so gentle then
so giving
so peaceful
hiding all the darkness stuffing it down
pretending convincing birth canceled out death

We dreamt together
became soul mates
inspired each other
on our path built with hope and conviction
believing when faith was gone

Images of threes dance forth.
I hear your cries in my dreams
I sweat out your fears
praying to fend off the madness

I thought I was crazy when I started to see visions
they visit me
tell me everything
not knowing how to tap in the third eye with any clarity
I thought it was me
slipping into the locura of it all

but it is time
to listen

Armando Corazones

Libre mi canto Libre mi canto
Libre mi canto en vez del llanto
Bottom lips seeping in cavernous eyelids
Shaky heart, wicked body, liquid disappointment rushing through
Curious enough, passionate enough,
To keep on living.

Streets full of trickery, tiring by your side with paranoia
Will you be mistaken for the terrorist of the week?
Cuffed shoved provoked to fall
Why play the game when at random I will be made to play victim of the day?

And my traumatic nerves will jump at every heart.beat.
Intending to communicate
Libre mi canto Libre mi canto
Libre mi canto en vez del llanto

Chaos jumped out in the guise of a badge
And put my pacifist lover in a headlock
Threatening, my love, to take your last breath
Misunderstanding our civil discussion, arrested for speaking Spanish
Too passionately in an English-only zone.
Libre mi canto Libre mi canto
Libre mi canto en vez del llanto

Officer Serno you said, "I know in your country being macho is okay..."

But I had more fear of your legalized handcuffs pushing me, provoking me,
a school girl. But my citizenship doesn't make you understand
why I too light to be Latina would be with my brown man.
How come if concerned for my safety,
from this passionate peace loving man,

Me loving man,
You never asked me if I was okay?
If I was in trouble you reacted without asking me if I was okay?

The only bruises left from your un-aggravated brutality

"Are you on drugs?"
NO
"Have you been drinking?"
NO
Commented my lover could be a terrorist for all he knew.

Libre mi canto Libre mi canto
Libre mi canto en vez del llanto

Peace loving brothers and sisters
Recen por mí.
Muestrame la fuerza para enfrentar la discriminación
a hacer mis ideales mas fuertes
a usar mi pasión para el canto y el baile rico de la vida
a hablar con pocas pero poderosas palabras
a ayudarme a no volverme victima o ser insignificant, powerless
a encontrar la tranquilidad.
Deme el poder de cambiar el rancor a la paz interna.

Y deja
Libre mi canto Libre mi canto
Libre mi canto en vez del llanto

Voy a armar mi corazón
Voy a armar mi corazón
Voy armar mi corazón y libre voy a ser.

Thirst

eyelashes handsome blink hello
concha drips come take a sip
taste earth as clouds part
ground thirsting for first rain
we burn leña old school for tortillas in adobe

rivers drip down my chest
after hours days years and too many seconds of flesh at rest
gritos of bliss breathe life
a homegirl thirsty
beber de tu fuente me quita la sed
quítamelo y dámelo
tienta
birds of paradise extravagant dance
dice
ándale mamacita que no quieres?

Red Puta Heels and the Joker

she had a novela moment
all *Dos Mujeres, Un Camino*

prevented it from getting tragic
kept her tacones dancing on her feet

instead of hurled through space
at your face

had already done her penance
called instead upon the locas

to work it out
on the dance floor

last night
the
dj saved

her
life

summoning the diosas in the club
to perform ceremony

warm her body
work it over

pledging allegiance to broken hearts everywhere
the risk she was willing to take

she got hers but wanted it to last longer
thought it would be different

all those projects and plans
thought she could step back and be friends

why didn't she listen to her intuition
why did you use her as your transition
why didn't you tell the truth

like at the beginning

you won't see her fall apart
you won't do that
to her

Más y Más

You're uncomfortable sometimes with the stares when we are in public
but I in all my femme glory

enjoy holding your hand,
showing affection in public with reckless abandon;

our simple presence a radical disruption of hetero-norm-ativi-ty
Each loving moment defies any concern

that we are both worthy of love
Caressing your cheek will be one of many simple revolutions

All this while each one of us continues on our own path
Open, building trust, free to express our needs, emotions, frustrations,

dreams, hopes and have some fun while we're at it
Friends   Allies   Radical lovers   Platonic or romantic

Love is love
And we all could use more of it

Showing up

I gave green light kisses on her eyelashes
to confirm that we were
birthed from memory.
romantic she told me when I wasn't next to her que:
"tú me haces mucha falta."
instead of swooning
I translate literally
"I find you missing."

Worried I am her lack I say
"why don't you go save the stars?"
Running so I don't have to face what's in between.

Sick from the potential I lost her
stuck in the twisted reflection of my misery
I missed her.
caught between the shoulds. If then. Should have
means harder.
My heart valves flicker, lungs reach
capacity praying for more chest space.
the fight means releasing.
Imperfect beautiful should
confront the magic instead of wanting to flee.

Writer meets air. showing up. fist open.
essential intention. not your savior.
destroying the foundation 'cause
it's beneath you. shades people carry
as symbolic offering.

mind
lost.
again.

not speaking 'cause of a message too fly to catch.
a contract to cut the junk food lines.
leave laziness behind
even when she gets fast on you.

We here
forming a ritual that helps bring out the truth.
defense shield behind. strength and wisdom
to gather more strength and wisdom.
Redemption transforms I hear.
the honesty in the poet circle is what informs the heart broken.

If I could see her again I would say
thank you for permission.
seeing the god in me when I most wanted to disappear
for tools that work outside this room.
especially for holding silence.
for releasing sweaty palms pushing.
no control over uncomfortable
story.

I am working on betrayed definitions.
a narrowing. a moment that happened before.
staying away from short term symptom relief.
Asking the same questions hoping for no answers. the story remains
a glimmer. that way you learn
and for the sake of all we'll retire the use of ancestors as a crutch
quit enabling their dysfunction in the afterlife.
bridging slow with tools from the magic room.

A poet in recovery.

Nuestras Utopías

I wish I could sign up for punctual intellectual embodied knowledge pep talks, instant messages, texts, email blasts or home visits
like signing up for daily horoscopes.

Then maybe I could slash and dash through the (parenthetical) identity spaces of hyphenated -name -calling and come up with daily transnational decolonized dance moves that reinvigorate our daily missions.

I wish I got more hugs in a day and that respectful eye contact were a given.

I wish we could engage at each other's levels until everyone felt heard but barely said a word and you wouldn't interrupt my stutter because you think you know better.

I wish I could space-time travel to the exact locations where I am wanted, needed, effective and to simply bear witness.

I wish loneliness would quit arguing with intimacy about silence and make amends with time.

I wish the burden of discipline came out in syncopated song harmonies even when the clouds hide the sun.

I wish polite anger and so-called irrational outbursts could double date with guilty repressed self-hate and recognized privilege.

I wish revolutionary self-care was a required subject in high school.

I wish I could remember love is what I was born to do.

I wish I could eat your tears with rainbow kisses and quench my thirst for eight daily glasses of balance, self-determination and growth.

I wish I could archive our knowledge of pain, self-destruction and manifest destiny, to revisit only when I needed a reminder of how far we've come.

I wish everyone got credit for the work they've done and extra credit for fleeting thoughts, mediation, meditation and verbs that bridge the chasms.

I wish I had a magic glitter-filled pen to write in the names where the documents left you out over and over until everyone had their say, exhausting possibilities, taking a union break for healthy snacks and structured consensual affection.

I wish we weren't in competition with crumbs and that we could form a new Voltron-being anytime we needed to call on each other's powers.

I wish intellect didn't make emotions feel less than.

I wish I could give degrees in harmony, spirit and collective progress and that I knew my story like I know theirs.

I wish I didn't lose my breath when I need to speak my truth.

I wish hibernation didn't draw attention to your absence.

I wish the powerful had to play rainy day games to remind them that they are small.

I wish lovemaking gave birth to the earth's breath evenly distributing health, sustenance and star shine to those who are hungry in the love vacuum.

I wish the insights of prisoners could engineer release valves amid hierarchy towers where pressed chests gasp for breath.

I wish we were required to renew ceremony every time like car registrations, library books or TV seasons.

I wish that status was less about pulling rank and that updates were more that created shelter from the norm's storm.

I wish I could draw mathematical equations out of recycled materials that gave us all we need.

I wish I could say, dance, sing all the insight, vision, flesh, document you need to hear, see, touch, be.

Afterword

by Karina Oliva Alvarado, Ph.D., Visiting Lecturer
Chicana and Chicano Studies Department
University of California, Los Angeles

From where do dreams emerge? For Maya Chinchilla, they emerge from a nexus of exquisite beauty from "Guate,\ Place of Trees" found in the intersected images of Guatemala, D.F. Mexico, MacArthur Park L.A., and the Mission District, S.F. Each of these are experiences rather than places. Each contains a home and a rupture. We are made to feel each as a place of foreign belonging. To read Chinchilla's poems is to dream itself and while dreaming to ask, is this my dream or is this a dream I can share with you?

Rather than to situate oneself in the stable ground of marginality and exclusion, Chinchilla's words shift with inquiry of the person between lands and identities, of the person cognizant of her own power and agency and yet struggling with the disparities embedded in all relations of power-state, sexual, linguistic, familial.

In this way, rather than ask what happens to a dream deferred, Maya Chinchilla asks, in the context of struggle, how can we not dream? She seduces: dream with me and I will share with you my sensual world. As a people whose very presence is questioned, as a Central American, a queer woman, a poet with many languages and cultural codes, Chinchilla's poetry coaxes us to dream and imagine beyond our limits into the fanciful worlds of the "Central American Unicorn"-the mythic place some of us are made to occupy through our exile from the normative and ideal worlds of American hegemony and the extremities of Central America.

So begins her questioning. How can Central Americans and U.S. Central Americans locate ourselves in a continental imagination that polarizes and elevates the North from the South while excluding the lands and cultures in between languages, sexes, continents, nations, bodies, and imaginations. This contradictory and poignant space emerges in her poem, "Central American American" where her poetic voice oscillates between indignant statements of the knowing exile, and the migrant seeking help,

"America
América
Las Américas
Español chapín"

"they tell us the American dream is the truth
but that our stories of escape from horror are not"

"show me where my home is"

"am I CENTRAL
American?
Where is the center of America?"

While seeking validation of one's history, culture and presence and of one's own Chapín language, Chinchilla does not surrender the act of dreaming to North America only. Through the simple, yet very conscious act of not capitalizing Dream after American, the American Dream loses its mythic power as the great signifier and motivator to a better life. While hegemony remains an abstract that validates its own truth value, placing "our stories of escape" in contrast to the truth of the American dream, Chinchilla ends up destabilizing truth as inherent, while highlighting the erasure, and horror, underlying the myth of American progress. Through direct language, Chinchilla highlights the poetics of self-representing the selves that all social normatives seek to standardize, restrict, deny, and shadow.

How can one have a sense of home and direction when one's presence is outside the margins? The need to have a home and to be at home, the need to belong, also becomes a challenge since "show me where my home is" can be an ironical request, the idea that a stranger to one's very existence knows better, can actually tell us where we belong. This is a critical and conflicted question for 1.5 and second generation Central Americans who theoretically exist in the center as U.S. inhabitants and yet, whose limited cultural visibility continues to undermine their particular multidimensional experiences, identities, and communities.

Do not allow Chinchilla's playful and colorful language deceive you as in her poem, "No Nonsense Grand Ma Goddess, "I dreamt of her smooth hair permanent wave set / pink lipstick click tongue clip-on costume jewelry polyester pant suits" for underlying the scents, colors, textures, rhythms and musicality in her work, is a dedicated poetic crafting complex theoretical questions that get to the heart of being Maya Chinchilla. In fact, her poem, "Central American American" inspired the language within academia to explore U.S. Central Americans as a distinctly specific nexus of subjectivities-Central Americans born and or raised in the United States. That is the power of her language; her work is that influential.

This moving, powerful, and playful book of poems and narratives are a historical moment for U.S. Central Americans. It has certainly been long awaited. However, the magic of Chinchilla's work is that it welcomes all of us to dream and to dream together. So by no means should this book be limited only within queer, or U.S. Central American, or Guatemalan communities. The book's complex intertext is already in dialog with multiple cultures that are part of our American landscape. Share in the transformation that expands Martí's Nuestra América to "Nuestras Utopias" as an ongoing dream of betterment and justice that belongs to us all.

About Maya Chinchilla

Maya Chinchilla is a Guatemalan, Bay Area-based writer, video artist, and educator with an MFA in English and Creative Writing from Mills College. She writes and performs poetry that explores themes of historical memory, heartbreak, tenderness, sexuality, and alternative futures. Her work —sassy, witty, performative, and self-aware— draws on a tradition of truth-telling and poking fun at the wounds we carry.

Born and raised in Long Beach, CA, by a mixed class, mixed race, immigrant activist extended family, Maya has lived and loved in the Bay Area for the second half of her life. Her work has been published in anthologies and journals including: *Mujeres de Maíz, Sinister Wisdom, Americas y Latinas: A Stanford Journal of Latin American Studies, Cipactli Journal,* and *The Lunada Literary Anthology*, and is quoted (and misquoted) in essays, presentations and books on U.S.-Central American poetics; Chicana/Latina literature; and identity, gender, and sexuality.

Maya is a founding member of the performance group Las Manas, a former artist-in-residence at Galería de La Raza in San Francisco, CA, and La Peña Cultural Center in Berkeley, CA, and is a VONA Voices and Dos Brujas workshop alum. She is the co-editor of *Desde El Epicentro: An anthology of Central American Poetry and Art* and is a lecturer at San Francisco State University.

OTHER KÓRIMA PRESS TITLES

Amorcito Maricón
      by Lorenzo Herrera y Lozano

The Beast of Times
      by Adelina Anthony

Brazos, Carry Me
      by Pablo Miguel Martínez

Ditch Water: Poems
      by Joseph Delgado

Empanada: A Lesbiana Story en Probaditas
      by Anel I. Flores

Las Hociconas: Three Locas with Big Mouths and Even Bigger Brains
      by Adelina Anthony

Joto: An Anthology of Queer Xicano & Chicano Poetry
      edited by Lorenzo Herrera y Lozano

Jotos del Barrio
      by Jesús Alonzo

The Possibilities of Mud
      by Joe Jiménez

Tragic Bitches: An Experiment in Queer Xicana & Xicano Performance Poetry
      by Adelina Anthony, Dino Foxx, and Lorenzo Herrera y Lozano

When the Glitter Fades
      by Dino Foxx

Made in the USA
Coppell, TX
02 February 2022

72866660R00080